FERDINARD S LAWSON

152

MIND SUPPLEMENTS
FOR WEALTH CREATION

FERDINARD S LAWSON

152

MIND SUPPLEMENTS
FOR WEALTH CREATION

MEMOIRS

Cirencester

Published by Memoirs

MEMOIRS
PUBLISHING

Memoirs Books

25 Market Place, Cirencester, Gloucestershire, GL7 2NX
info@memoirsbooks.co.uk www.memoirspublishing.com

Copyright ©Ferdinard S Lawson, January 2013
First published in England, January 2013
Book jacket design Ray Lipscombe

ISBN 978-1-909544-10-9

Printed in England

FERDINARD SENYO LAWSON

ABOUT THE AUTHOR

Ferdinard S. Lawson served as an armour bearer for many years to the senior pastor and founder of the House of Judah Praise Ministries, Bishop Dr. Michael Hutton-Wood. Prior to that, the author served some senior pastors in the capacity of an armour bearer in Ghana, especially during his service in the Deeper Life Bible Church. Ferdinard's mandate is to empower, motivate and encourage believers to remain focused in serving the Lord. Presently, he lives in London (UK) with his wife and their two lovely children.

ABOUT THIS BOOK

ARE YOU THINKING YOURSELF RICHER?

This book is designed to provide the reader with the necessary mind supplements for wealth creation. The mind is the storehouse for great inventions and the Earth can only yield its full increase to you when you engage its power.

This book will stimulate your mind to:

- **Discover and develop your talents to enable yourself to add value to people.**
- **Learn to appreciate the value of time for wealth creation.**
- **Develop a leadership mindset.**
- **Learn about some mind deficiencies you must avoid.**

And you will learn much more. Receiving the right supplements from this book will stimulate your mind to achieve its full power to enhance your productivity and fight against any deficiency which is preventing your creative mind from working harder to provide ideas for wealth creation. In view of this the mind need some supplements to enable it to work effectively to generate the full potential to create your wealth in life.

DEDICATION

I want to dedicate this book to the Lord God Almighty, who through His creative power and wisdom created me and enabled me to contribute to my knowledge and wisdom to my generation and the generation to come. Thank you LORD.

I am also dedicating this book to all men and women who have contributed positively to the world we live in now by unlocking the secrets of the mind. These men have left legacies for us to follow so that we can continue to influence our world productively through the power of wealth creation

Finally to my parents, Mr and Mrs Lawson, my wife, children and siblings. May Almighty God multiply and increase you all on every side in Jesus' name.

ACKNOWLEDGEMENTS

My sincere thanks go to my destiny father Rev Dr Bishop Michael Hutton-Wood, himself a writer and the founder of the House of Judah (PRAISE) Ministries Worldwide with the mandate to raise generational leaders to impact nations by empowering men and women to release their full potential and maximize their destiny.

I express my profound gratitude to Rev Dr Paul Yaw Frimpong-Manso (General Superintendent of the General Council of Assemblies of God, Ghana) for his prayers and encouragement to bring this book to reality. May God richly bless you.

I want to express my sincere gratitude to my spiritual mentor pastor Charles Owusu (Deeper Christian Life Bible Church, Ghana). You are a great inspiration to me and my family both here in the United Kingdom and in Ghana. God bless you!

But thou shalt remember the LORD thy God: for it is he that giveth thee power to get wealth that he may establish his covenant which he sware unto thy fathers, as it is this day. Deuteronomy 8:18

Beloved, I wish above all things that thou mayest prosper and be in health, even as thy soul prospereth

3 John 1:2

INTRODUCTION

Our thoughts influence our existence, and our environment depends on how we set our mind to see positive results. In fact our happiness or unhappiness depends on whether our thoughts are positive or negative. Ultimately, our individual minds predict whether or not we will fulfill our potential and have an impact on nations.

There are two sides of your brain, the left and right. The left side is where logic and very detailed processes are executed. The right side contains your creativity and imagination. Over time, people tend to develop one side of the brain more than the other and rely on the side they are most comfortable with. It takes just a few mind supplements to stimulate and fight against any form of deficiency between the left and right side of your creative mind.

NOTE: If you are lacking in ideas, useful suggestions and plans and the finger of God touches you, your creative abilities will suddenly receive a boost. Are you short of ideas that can give your business or church a positive turnaround? The finger of God will touch you and what you lacked shall be created. As the Lord touches you today, everything that is lacking in your ministry, finances and family shall come into being. They shall be created. Ask that the finger of God touches you today. Release your faith and expect the impossible but desirable to take place. Your situation is about to change for the best as your mind is stimulated for wealth creation, in Jesus' Name AMEN!

1. Wealth creators are paid more because they are creative thinkers. Decorated life is a by-product of a creative mind.

2. Wealth creators are individuals who discover projects and shake their world.

3. The world cannot exist without creative-minded people.

4. Creative people and wealth generators are those who pay the price for greatness.

5. Creative minds focus on the precious future and are not satisfied with their present condition.

6. You create your wealth by investing in the small ideas you have to produce a greater harvest.

7. Wealth creators appreciate the value of time they spend alone without feeling lonely.

8. A creative mind seizes each moment and never allows others to steal precious time.

9. Tiredness and retirement are two diseases which affect the creative mind.

10. Thinkers are those who don't allow fear of failure to stop them trying something new.

11. Wealth creators don't wait for things to happen to them – they take advantage of problems and solve them.

12. Wealth creators are those who don't wait for ideal conditions but examine themselves to change their surroundings.

13. Wealth creators work as if they owned the company they work in, even if they are new staff.

14. Positive and productive thinkers are wealth creators because they have the mindset of possibility in everything they do.

15. People who are immune to all forms of negative criticism are wealth creators who take the world by storm.

16. Humble people are wealth creators because they do not fight people for credit due to them and are never over-ambitious.

17. Creative-minded people have the spirit of flexibility as they tend to adjust to unexpected challenges in order to obtain maximum results.

18. Wealth creators are those who avail themselves of new skills to make themselves marketable.

19. Wealth creators are those who see great treasures in trash and know that God is all they need to have all their needs met.

20. You can only create your wealth by taking the bricks thrown at you to lay a solid foundation for the release and fulfilment of your destiny.

21. Wealth creators are those who chase their purpose in life and do not rely on their pensions for subsistence.

22. Creative-minded people take full responsibility when things go wrong and devise ways of correcting problems instead of blaming others for their indiscipline and failures.

23. Wealth creators are those who appreciate God-given talents and use them to add value to mankind.

24. Wealth creators are those who value other people's involvement to achieve a common goal. They appreciate that others have a role to contribute to their success.

25. Wealth creators set high standards and do everything possible to break old ones, because they believe in excellence.

26. Creative-minded people and wealth creators are those who believe in the spirit of team building.

27. Wealth creators know that schooling gives you a certificate to look for work, but taking the mind supplements enables them to have an advantage over others.

28. Sometimes the only person you have to beat to get to the finishing line is YOU.

29. Hard work and dedication are the main supplements needed for the actualization of your gifts and talents embedded within you.

30. People will laugh with you, not at you, when you ignite the power of your creative mind to solve people problems. Are you a candidate to add value?

31. The creative mind you ignite is what God gave you to generate your wealth in life.

32. A person with no skills or experience is not a lot of use to an employer - until they ignite the power of their creative thinking to add value.

33. A true leader is one who wins people's trust and shows them that what they can do is the sure way to help encourage others to become themselves.

34. Being small-minded about something in life prevents an individual from achieving greater things or rising above boundaries.

35. A wealth creator only dwells on positive and productive things. They understand that negative and fruitless thoughts result in less production.

36. Wealth creators discover themselves before they are discovered by somebody else. This gives them the platform to stand on to achieve something greater in life, because knowing yourself influences your self-esteem, personality and wellbeing.

37. Wealth creators are individuals who believe that lack of self-discovery and renewing of their mindset makes an individual depressed and can sometimes leads to suicidal thoughts, simply because they have become frustrated about life and are not engaging the power of the creative mind to do something profitable with their personal life.

38. Wealth creators know that the secret of their future is hidden in their daily routine, so they are careful about what occupies their mind because it will determine what they become tomorrow.

39. Wealth creators appreciate the gifts and talents they have discovered in themselves and look for an opportunity to use those talents to add value to people.

40. Wealth creators have discovered that their provision, protection and promotion lie in their purpose in life through creative thinking.

41. Be mindful of your associations, because they determine your success in life.

42. Your standard of living does not depend on your geographical location but the creative mind you used in creating your wealth.

43. Wealth creators are potential thinkers and potential achievers, because they see great opportunity and potential in life.

44. How hot is your mind or your brain? It determines how high your salary will be in life.

45. Wealth creators are those who create rules and manuals and determine the sphere of their lives.

46. Wealth creators are very mindful of their thoughts, because they know that their thought is a mental cheque for the payment of their destiny.

47. Your destiny does not depends on what you eat or see but on what you invest in with your creative mind.

48. Every leader has a level of influence based on the level of quality information they have.

49. Who you surround yourself with determines what will gravitate towards you in life. So watch your associations.

50. Small-minded people talk about people, but large-minded people talk about how to create their wealth.

51. Your attitude in times of difficulties and challenges determines how you go through the challenge.

52. Knowing yourself gives you the power to be confident that nobody is like you by igniting the power of your creative mind to add value to men.

53. Because of the level of your greatness you may have to go through some challenging experiences.

54. You can only design your destiny by seeing treasures in the trash heaped on you.

55. True leaders are those who have taken the bricks thrown at them and used them to lay a solid foundation for the fulfilment of their sure destiny.

56. Remember that pursuing your dreams requires daring to be different, even making radical changes to see that those dreams come true.

57. A leader's purpose and mission determines his or her lifestyle, attention and the battles he has to fight.

58. Leaders are known for what they do and not who they are. They spend more time producing results than attempting to boost their egos.

59. Do not focus so much on the challenges and problems you are faced with daily that you lose the sight of God's grace and presence in you.

60. Your mission and purpose in life are vital. Without your contribution your generation is going nowhere.

61. Leaders should not be excessively secretive, claiming that they are only accountable to God. Motives and action must be cleared' - Eastwood Anaba

62. You do not become a record breaker until you break a record.

63. You do not become breaking news until you become news by using the gifts and talent you have.

64. Don't allow the questions people ask you to make you sad; always remain calm and positive in your response.

65. You are no one but yourself, so do not do what everyone else is doing. Discover what is special to your purpose in life and do it.

66. In life never allow your situation to change your standard of living - use your standard of living to change your situation.

67. A leader's attitude will either increase or decrease the team's ability to influence the capital market.

68. Your level of breakthrough is determined by the level at which you discover yourself.

69. Your future can only shrink or expand in the same proportion to the level of courage you demonstrate as an individual - not as a group.

70. 'It does not really matter where one is born but who one is born' - Bishop Alex Mwami

71. You can never be unbeatable unless you can beat your lazy self.

72. Your position in life is based on the foundation of the talent you build on. Do not bury your talent but rather use it to change lives.

73. Any leader who refuses to say SORRY should never expect SORRY from others. What you sow is what you reap.

74. Determination and dedication are the two ingredients most needed to spice your dream.

75. Who says you weren't destined for greatness? Just ignite the power of your creative mind to use your talent to create your wealth in life.

76. Praise and criticism are two things which can motivate an individual into greatness, depending on the mindset one cultivates.

77. Your progress and success in life is based on your connectivity with the people whom God brings your way. Be mindful of recommendations.

78. 'If you cannot laugh any more you cannot love any more. So check the level at which you laugh' - Bishop Akoto Bamfo

79. Life is not void of signposts. Just depend on God for the direction of your life.

80. Always celebrate those who celebrate your success after they have contributed to your discovering your potential in life.

81. You must avoid the company of those who do not in any way share your vision or have your interests at heart.

82. Be mindful of what you think, because it will determine the next level of your trade in life.

83. When you are in demand you make demands. So develop yourself to be in demand.

84. You don't get paid for doing nothing. You do not make a living by what you get but by what you give.

85. Another man's failures cannot determine or predict your success in the future.

86. The platform you stand on will either make you or break you. So watch the platform you stand on.

87. Your value of knowledge determines your next level in life.

88. 'I learned a lot about the people around me today. The good ones stayed and the bad ones left.' Avoid dream killers in your destiny.

89. Never hate people who are jealous of you, but respect their jealousy because they're the ones who think you're better than them.

90. Wealth creators don't think they are that perfect but trust God for his grace.

91. Wealth creators don't need money to generate creative ideas, but you need a creative mind to generate money.

92. Wealth creators only see their disability as their potential ability to create their wealth.

93. You may be feeling more confident about who you are and what you say. The power of self-discovery is what makes you do what you do.

94. Wealth creators are driven by defined purpose and don't allow the colour of their skin to stop them achieving their destiny.

95. If your enemy enjoys the rate at which you sleep and snore, then your destiny has been taken away from you without you knowing.

96. Your ability to handle small matters will determine your ability to handle greater responsibilities.

97. Don't give up on yourself. Grades don't define intelligence and age doesn't define maturity.

98. When people cut you down or talk behind your back, remember that they took time out of their pathetic lives, just to think about you.

99. No lazy man can follow the steps of a successful and hardworking person until his mind is transformed.

100. If you are afraid of becoming different you can never make a difference.

101. No matter how many mistakes you make or how slow your progress, you are still way ahead of everyone who isn't trying.

102. The power of association tells you that the stars need the moon to contribute to their radiation.

103. Your dream is what gives credibility to your living. What are you here for? What are you adding to the world? How much impact are you making?

104. Your dream in life is what determines the amount of sleep you get. Your dream should intercept your sleeping level.

105. Do not use people to achieve your dream and discard them along the way. Don't be a talent abuser.

106. Wealth creators do not walk by the flesh – if you do so you will sink, but if you walk by faith and lead by the spirit you will float above your situations.

107. Wealth creators value the roles of mentors in their lives and believe that without a role model in your life you cannot play your role well.

108. Believe in yourself: We must believe in ourselves or no one else will believe in us. 'We must match our aspirations with the competence, courage and determination to succeed' - Rosalyn Sussman Yalow, US medical physicist. The Bible said David encouraged himself in the Lord and kept reminding himself of who God is and who his children are – 1 Samuel 30:6 David was discouraged because of an enemy who was jealous of him and tried to destroy him. Are there people in your life who are consciously trying to do you harm? Are there some people close to you who are jealous, mean or vindictive? That can be very discouraging. *Oh, that I had wings of a dove! David wrote; I would fly away and be at rest - I would hurry to my place of shelter, far from the tempest and storm (Psalm 55:5-6).* What do you say to yourself when you are discouraged? Do you speak more discouraging words to yourself? Let us make a sacrifice of praise unto the Lord and worship him with thanksgiving, and in the process of time the Heavenly Father who gives good gifts to his children will definitely show up in the midst of your circumstances.

109. Dwell in God's word daily: *'Let the word of Christ dwell in you richly in all wisdom; teaching and admonishing one another in psalms and hymns and spiritual songs, singing with grace in your hearts to the Lord' - Colossian 3:16*

Romans 15:4 informs us that everything that was written in the past was written to teach us, so that through endurance and the encouragement of the scriptures we might have hope. Make yourself get into the word of God even if it seems dry and lifeless to you. Keep reading and you will be encouraged and uplifted. When we allow God's Word to dwell in our lives, it changes and transforms us into the image of God himself. It also becomes treasured in our lives. *'All Scripture is given by inspiration of God, and is profitable for doctrine, for reproof, for correction, for instruction in righteousness, that the man of God may be complete, thoroughly equipped for every good work'* - 2 Timothy 3:16. Furthermore, the word of God allows us to drop off all negative things that disturbed us at one time, and in many cases, overcame us. Amazingly, the word of God makes you healthy in your physical appearance with the glory of the Lord shining in your face. Meditating on God's word creates calmness in your inner spirit and even eliminates or reduces the symptoms of many illnesses.

'Do not let this Book of the Law depart from your mouth; meditate on it day and night, so that you may be careful to do everything written in it. Then you will be prosperous and successful'. – Joshua 1:8 (New International Version)

110. Use your talent in God's House: One other way of addressing your own discouragement is to motivate others. Proverbs 11:25: 'He who refreshes others will himself/herself be refreshed'. Instead of looking for someone to pick you up, look around to see who *you* can pick up. Thank goodness, we can be motivators even when we feel discouraged and in the process of time you may become a motivator and lessen your own need.

'Not forsaking the assembling of ourselves together, as the manner of some is; but exhorting one another; and so much the more, as ye see the day approaching.' - Hebrews 10:25

One good cure for discouragement is simply to get involved in church activities. Find a department within your church and be committed and loyal to it. This may encourage and change your moods. At times when we are discouraged we become frustrated, unmotivated and let down, but as you join forces with other believers to undertake God's work, you will become motivated and encouraged and of course uplifted, overcoming fear and anxiety.

Spend some time in the fellowship of those people with strong faith, share the word of God and meditate on the word. We need to get together more often, even in the midst of our busy lives, because we need each other to stay encouraged. Encouragement is one of the most important things we all need and expect when we are discouraged or feeling down. That is why in Jude 1:19-2, the Bible says 'But you, beloved, building yourselves up on your most holy faith, praying in the Holy Spirit, (21) keep yourselves in the love of God, looking for the mercy of our Lord Jesus Christ unto eternal life.'

We need positive and productive people in our lives to motivate us to keep pressing on in the faith, to build us in the Christian journey so that we do not lose hope but keep on the course and stay alert. It takes self discipline and self motivation to bring us close to God. Therefore, it is very important that we know the Word.

Galatians 6:1 educates us that '*Brethren, if a man is overtaken in any trespass, you who are spiritual restore such a one in a spirit of gentleness, considering yourself lest you also be tempted.'* This is to say that trying to stand alone without a good fellowship with other Christian brethren can bring you face to face with discouragement.

111. Wealth creators have the spirit of sincerity. They are very sincere in their actions. Don't try to deceive or impress others. Be yourself, and do what you feel is right based on your values and beliefs. You will be surprised at how people accept you when you stop trying to be someone you are not.

112. Productive people and wealth creators are genuine in whatever they do; their actions speak louder than their words. Don't falsify or embellish events that may have happened. Don't say one thing and do the other.

113. To be a wealth creator you need to be wholehearted. You need to be very enthusiastic about what you do. Show it. Be committed to life and everything you set out to accomplish in life. Devote yourself to your family, friends, and community and commit yourself to being the best father, husband, wife, mother, friend and neighbour you can be.

114. Creators of wealth are very honest individuals. They never use fraud or deception to get ahead in life.

115. Wealth creators don't go through life thinking they are better than others or superior to those around them. They are able to interact equally with everyone who comes their way.

116. Always follow your heartfelt values, and never let a situation or person steer you away from doing what you know is right. Be someone who people can look up to and respect and not someone who trades his or her moral values for material gains in life.

117. Let it be known that you stand firm for what you believe in and that your morals, values and actions are not for sale. Don't let outside forces corrupt the person you are.

118. Show good judgment and sense in life. Don't let prejudices or emotions cloud your judgment.

119. Be focused on what you want to achieve in life. Give everyone you interact with your complete and undivided attention.

120. Practise good manners even though others around you may not.

121. Graciousness and respect go a long way in life. What is more, they are viral – when people see you doing it they are more apt to practise civility themselves.

Be kind to others and extend courtesy towards them. Don't interrupt people when they speak and don't dominate the conversation.

122. Gain from the wisdom that is inside you. Understand the inner qualities of people and learn how to understand situations that might be different from those we are used to.

123. Practise kind, gentle, and compassionate treatment of others – especially those who may be undeserving. Learn to extend a hand to help others, even though they themselves may not have helped you.

124. Be aware that each person is different and may have different values and beliefs from those you hold. Be understanding of the feelings and thoughts of others without having to be told or reminded of them.

125. Share your feelings with others and understand the emotional situations people go through. Put yourself in their shoes.

126. When someone is in distress, reach out with a genuine interest in helping to alleviate their suffering.

127. Think of others without thinking of yourself. Do good things for people without expecting something in return for yourself.

128. Be generous in life. Give of your time, money and wisdom. Share with others so they can see the true joy and adventures of life themselves.

129. Wealth creators spend less than they earn and invest the remainder wisely for their future.

130. Wealth creators have the habit of thinking rich. They believe that what they think is what they can have.

131. Wealth creators are ready to share their skills to help others and that enhance their own skill.

132. Most often wealth creators do the thing they fear most to change their perspective about things.

133. A creative mind enables you to take reasonable risks to see the change you want in life.

134. Wealth creators read about other successful people to change their thoughts and use their stories as guides.

135. Wealth creators keep up to date with the latest research on health, beauty and intelligence. Only those whose thoughts keep searching will stay intelligent for life.

136. Wealth creators usually go where challenges are and avoid comfort zones.

137. Wealth creators have the spirit of discernment. This enables them to avoid evil traps set by the enemies of progress.

138. Wealth creators are people who take the initiative to raise capital for growth. They think about how to influence the global market by not limiting their creative ideas.

139. To be a wealth creator, you need to live by your own principles and not allow emotions to override your judgment.

140. Wealth creators ensure that they live by what they teach others. They do not live a double life to fool others.

141. Self-development is what enables you to have confidence in igniting your creative mind to create your desired wealth

142. The power of your creative mind helps you to create your own work rather than working for somebody else.

143. Poverty is not eradicated through shouting and praying against problems but by engaging the creative mind to deal with the root cause.

144. The only different between the rich and the poor person is the creative mindset.

145. A creative mind leads to creative wealth. Develop your mind for your change of status.

146. Begin to change your thinking, not to need money but to create money through your creative mind (Romans 12: 1-2).

147. Slavery does not stop until your mind is stimulated to create your change your circumstances.

148. A stimulated mind is one that has many options to create money rather than relying on only one source of income.

149. A creative mind eradicates racism and sexism and gives the individual the power to be above all limitation.

150. A stimulated mind creates wealth irrespective of the geographical location. It is not limited to one location.

151. Wealth creators are those that make their mind sweat to produce what they want to see in their lives.

152. A Creative mind is the only way to withstand and overcome the whiplash of poverty.

SOME DEFICIENCIES YOU MUST AVOID

Deficiency occurs when the body lack some vital nutrients or vitamins from the food we eat. These deficiencies sabotage an individual's ability to generate wealth. Let's take a look at each of the most common deficiencies, the consequences and how to overcome them.

DEFICIENCY ONE: BURYING YOUR TALENT

Burying something means disposing of it, hiding it away or covering it with earth. In this context, I am advising how not to dispose, hide away or cover gifts and talents that God had endowed you with before you were born.

Gift and talent are not limited only to what you are good at but the passion or desire to accomplish that particular thing in life regardless of limitations and bring yourself fulfillment and happiness. Any gift or talent that does not bring you fulfilment in life is actually *not* your gift or talent.

The Merriam-Webster online dictionary defines talent as 'a characteristic feature, aptitude, or disposition of a person, the natural endowments of a person and a special, often athletic, creative, or artistic aptitude'.

We sometimes limit ourselves in many ways, which makes it impossible to appreciate the importance of the gifts and talent God has created us with. This might even tempt you to hide your talent. The question here is: why do people hide or bury their talent in the first place? I have discovered that people may want to bury their talents and gifts because of fear of failure. This can be a limitation to your wealth creation.

The bible says in Deuteronomy 31:8 that it *'will not fail or forsake you. Do not fear or be dismayed'*

'In his grace, God has given us different gifts for doing certain things well. So if God has given you the ability to prophesy, speak out with as much faith as God has given you'
(Romans 12:6).

Fear places limitations in your life and hinders you from getting to your desired future. The devil uses your limitation to move you away focusing on God's word concerning you. Do not limit yourself from getting to your destiny. Whatever gift or talent you have, begin to take the step of faith and do something with that talent and you will see the salvation of God in your life.

A gift unrewarded is a gift unused

Don't lose your enthusiasm about how to use your talent, do not bury that gift in yourself or hide it because of what people might have said concerning it. It does not matter what you have been through, the disappointments, setbacks or unjust treatment. I want to encourage you to believe that there is still something more for you to achieve and therefore you are above all limits. You may have been pushed down by family members or people around you for a time, but you will arise above your limitation.

'Rejoice not against me, O mine enemy: when I fall, I shall arise; when I sit in darkness, the Lord shall be a light unto me'

Micah 7:8

'Then he which had received the one talent came and said, Lord, I knew thee that thou art an hard man, reaping where thou hast not sown, and gathering where thou hast not strawed: And I was afraid, and went and hid thy talent in the earth: lo, there thou hast that is thine. His lord answered and said unto him, Thou wicked and slothful servant, thou knewest that I reap where I sowed not, and

gather where I have not strawed: Thou oughtest therefore to have put my money to the exchangers, and then at my coming I should have received mine own with usury. Take therefore the talent from him, and give it unto him which hath ten talents'

Matthew25:25-28

Every human being born on this earth has a talent. It does not matter how small that talent may look, it is still a talent that God has given you. But the question is: how many of us have actually discovered that talent within us? We saw in Matthew chapter 25:15, that the master, having discovered each person's strength, gift, capability and the ability in each of the servants, then gave them responsibilities, duties, role or talents matching their abilities and went straightway to his journey.

He was expecting to come back to hear good news about how each of the servants had used the talent and gifts he had given them. Therefore we can say that we are gifted or talented in one way or the other. The bible calls it 'ABILITY'. In Acts 11:29, the disciples were given talent, the ability to enable them to minister or send relief to the brethren which were in Judea.

Every talent that God has entrusted you with is to edify the body of Christ and to glorify Him, most importantly in the area of gifts and blessings imparted by the Holy Spirit. You need to acknowledge that each and every talent or ability that you have belongs to the Almighty God and therefore you have the responsibility to ensure that you use those talents in accordance to the purpose for which it has been given.

Paul the apostle in Romans chapter 12 verses 4-8 made it clear that each and every person is the recipient of every gift that they have and therefore when we come together in unity to contribute by using those gifts it will make a tremendous impact to the body of Christ. However, discovering talent is one thing and using that talent is another thing altogether. If you have a gift for singing and never have musical training to sharpen and develop that gift to add value to people, you are not using that gift and very soon you will lose that beautiful voice. You cannot blame the devil for making you lose that talent or gift of singing but yourself for not identifying the need for personal development. You may have the gift of serving, teaching, encouraging, contributing to the needs of others or leadership, you are suppose to use it to glorify God.

To succeed, you need to find something to hold on to, something to motivate you, something to inspire you - Tony Dorsett

Your life will always take shape when you use your talent and gifts. For example your career, family, ministry and community are improved when you use your God-given talent. Have you ever thought how powerful your talent or gift is? Have you sat down and asked yourself how an author becomes a best–seller? How about actors and actresses who have established themselves in the limelight? What about those businessmen who are earning millions by doing what they love and what they do best? You cannot say that you are gifted in playing football or running a hundred metres and not go for training and practice to be able to contest with the current world record holder (Usain Bolt) for the gold. You cannot be a winner that way. You have to discover yourself, discover your talent and be determined to use that talent maximally before that gift will be recognized and appreciated. You will experience and imagine the greater opportunities waiting out there for you if you choose to learn to use your talents.

Whatsoever thy hand findeth to do, do it with thy might; for there is no work, nor device, nor knowledge, nor wisdom, in the grave, whither thou goest. (Eccl 9.1)

Bob Marley once said that 'life is one big road with lots of signs so when you are riding through the ruts, difficult moments, challenges and fears, do not complicate your mind'. That is to say that you need to remain focused and endure hardship like a soldier on the battlefield. Do not bury your thoughts and your useful ideas.

The man with a new idea is a crank - until the idea succeeds - Mark Twain

Tell yourself that you are an inventor and your presence on earth is to create things that will add value to people. Remember that the days of inventing and being productive through the power of your creative mind are not over; many great and successful men and women did not bury their talents but believed the attitude of appreciating the small ideas in themselves and added skills to turn those ideas into inventions.

Rising above the limitations to your destiny can only be possible if you are determined and courageous enough to live and work smartly on your dreams and purposes for your life. Do not bury your talent under irresponsibility. Take responsibility for your destiny and with the help of God you will be all that He has created you to be. He created you in His image and commanded you to take dominion over creeping things. It is never too late to start using your talents.

'The future belongs to those who believe in the beauty of their dreams'

Eleanor Roosevelt

Don't bury it! In your hands you hold the seeds of failure or the potential for greatness. You can only create your desired wealth by focusing on the stars, even though things happening around might be limiting you. Begin to ignite the fire that is still burning in you and do not bury your talent.

Seeth thou a man diligent in his business, he shall stand before kings and shall not stand before mean men - (Proverbs 22:29)

Your talents can only bring light to mankind. Jesus Christ commanded us in Matthew 5: 14-16 to be the light of the world. What He was saying here is that our lives and talents should bring clarity to the world. Using your talent will demonstrate to the world how wonderful and creative your God is. The world will be under your feet when you use the talents God has created you with and do not bury it; it will bring light and dispel darkness and ignorance from people's lives and bring salvation to the dying world.

Irrespective of your size, every little gift or talent counts before God, just as a big fuel tanker carrying fuel to the deport needs a small amount of fuel to get to its destination.

Ferdinard S. Lawson

The lord is counting on you to start using your talents and gifts in singing, teaching the word, praying for the salvation of souls, nursing and caring for the sick and feeding the poor to bring restoration and revival to the generation. Don't be like the unwise servant who went and buried his talent in fear. You are here to take over, not to take cover. No matter how little or small you think your talent is, develop it and start using it to the glory of God. By so doing you will not be limited in your endeavours but God will make you a ruler over many things in Jesus Name.

DEFICIENCY TWO: PROCRASTINATION

**Go to the ant, you sluggard;
consider its ways and be wise!**

Proverbs 6:6

In pursuit of your destiny, you have the responsibility to ensure that everything you do drives you to that desired future. It is your duty to embrace time and let it be your best friend in your journey to your destiny.

No more limits to your destiny can only be a reality when

you acknowledge the power in your hands to change the way you approach things patterning to your future. One thing I have personally learned over the years is not to procrastinate – to put things off.

Developing the right attitude is all you need to be able to overcome the limitations of life. The late Zig Ziglar once said that 'others can stop you temporarily but you are the one who can stop yourself permanently'. This means that situations will try to limits your progress in life, but by developing the right attitude of not giving up in the midst of it all will enable you to overcome those limits and get to your destiny in Jesus Name.

To everything there is a season, and a time to every purpose under heaven: Ecclesiastes 3:1

There is time for everything we do and it is to your detriment that you waste time, because time does not wait for anyone. Therefore in this chapter, we are going to explore some of the reasons why we procrastinate, putting limits to our own progress in life. We also see some of the best ways of overcoming this killer of time.

Procrastination simply means to put off something that should be done in a particular time. This is one of the areas which affect many of us time after time.

In fact what differentiates a successful person from a failure is that successful individuals have the ability to recognize what, when, where, why and how to do something to add value to people around them. However, a failure may not even acknowledge that time is ticking by but leave everything to time and chance.

Whatever you may want to achieve and wherever you may want to get to, you have the power to get there through the grace of God, available to all mankind. Until you begin to take some action to fight any form of procrastination, this habit will only steals your opportunities, damage your career and pride or destroy your relationships and ministries.

'Procrastination is the thief of time'

- Edward Young

The word of God made an account in the book of Proverbs chapter 6:1-11; encouraging us to observe and acquire some vital knowledge from the ant.

Go to the ant, you sluggard; consider its ways and be wise! It has no commander, no overseer or ruler, yet it stores its provisions in summer and gathers its food at harvest. How long will you lie there, you sluggard? When will you get up from your sleep? A little sleep, a little slumber, a little folding of the hands to rest—and poverty will come on you like a bandit and scarcity like an armed man.

Proverbs 6:1-11

Sluggards are those who enjoy saying 'I will do it later, give me more time to rest' or 'A little sleep, a little slumber, a little folding of the hands to relax'. Each and every one of us faces the temptation to procrastinate. Don't we? We think that we can do something a bit later on and forget that the next thing to come to us is laziness.

The rate at which things are happening in the world today and the pressure to meet each demand may pose problems. Family life, college, work, employment meetings to attend and others are likely to drive you into the habits of procrastination. You may be giving excuses like 'I am waiting for the right time' or 'I am not in the right mood'. These are signs of procrastination which you need to check and avoid.

Many people have their own causes for procrastination, so you need to examine yourself to see what makes you feel lazy when it comes to doing something very important. These habits can be in the form of a lack of clear goals, underestimating the difficulty of the tasks and not being aware of the time required to complete the tasks. One of the main reasons why people tend to procrastinate is that they do not have a clear understanding of a particular task and may think that it has been imposed on them by somebody. Most often the fear of failure or fear of success is the reason why people are limited from getting to their desired destiny.

In the book 'How to defeat procrastination', Steven Cutler explained that procrastination is a behavioral problem. Most of the time people suffer its curse without realizing it is 'eating them alive'. Procrastination can make you unproductive, stressed and often guilty about the things you have failed to do. More importantly, it can cause people around you to dismiss you as uncooperative and obstructive to the group's progress. This now affects your social relations.

It is a sad fact that many of us have the tendency to procrastinate. Even though it is something that is regarded as unhelpful or even harmful, it may be very hard to find the strength within you not to yield to its temptation. However, keep in mind that overcoming procrastination is possible. It can be easy. You are strongly advised to cast out procrastination from your system if you are serious about getting to your destiny.

'You may delay, but time will not'
Benjamin Franklin

There are many ways to overcome the habit of procrastination in order to get to your destiny. It takes a spirit of concentration and commitment to actually overcome it. In fact you are simply wasting time which you could have used in building wealth, happiness and life contentment to add value to your generation.

The followings are some stair ladders to climb to overcome procrastination.

Ladders are used typically for reaching heights. When you are not tall enough to reach to such a height, the ladder is strategically placed to ensure safety. To climb over your limitations, you need the ladders to empower you to get to your height of destiny.

MOTIVATE YOURSELF

We read in proverbs 6:7 that the ants have no leaders or instructors to push them into greatness. That means they have to motivate themselves - *'no commander, overseer, or ruler'*. What is motivating you in life? What is your motivation in studying, working or serving God? Are you doing it because you think you have to do it? Doing what you do because someone told you to? Are you serving God because you are expecting a miracle from Him, or going to church because you do not want your church leaders to be calling you and asking you questions so you go to church to warm the benches?

What is driving you to do what you are doing in the first place? Let your motivation come from inside you as you read the word of God and not from the outside, pleasing men. My brethren, it doesn't depend on your situation, feelings or who you are working with or for. You may not be appreciated for what you may be doing for your employment, school, university, church, house, or family meetings, but you need to motivate yourself to keep the faith and press on to the prize waiting for you. Your salary may have been delayed by your boss, but as you are motivated to work hard and smartly, you will begin to see that you are progressing in life because what the enemy meant for evil, God will turn it to your favour.

It is interesting to know that the ants do not need anybody to motivate them. They do not need the Prime Minister, NATO or the United Nations to motivate them. Who are you waiting for to motivate you? Let the word of God motivate you in all you do. The bible said that when David returned from the land of the Philistines with his 600-man army to the village, Ziklag, upon arrival they saw that the Amalekites had invaded, burning their houses to the ground and kidnapping their wives and children. This horrible news caused David's small army to turn on him and talk of stoning him to death. With no one to lean to for advice, David could either give in or just accept his fate. One thing we know is that David was greatly distressed; for the people spoke of stoning him, because the soul of all the people was grieved, every man for his sons and for his daughters: but David encouraged (motivated) himself in the LORD his God.

Whatever you are doing, work at it with enthusiasm, as to the Lord and not for people!
Colossians 3:23

PLAN AHEAD

Planning ahead of time is one of the ladders needed to overcome procrastination. Planning ahead can help organize your day and your busy schedules. To be able to be all that the Lord has called you to and get to your destiny, planning ahead is a great way to prioritize and schedule those events and activities in a strategic manner.

No matter how busy your life, work, family and children are, you still need to plan ahead. Don't wait until the last minute. Or maybe you see others procrastinating until the last minute and it makes you worry that something will never get done in time. Regardless which of these profiles suits you, planning helps everyone work together while still getting everything done in a team.

From the passage we read in Proverbs 6:1-11, we discovered that the ants always plan ahead. We learned that they gather their food in preparation for the winter. They work hard during the summer when food supplies are abundant and can relax during the winter season, when food supplies are scarce.

Do you know when your 'summer' is and when your 'winter' is season to gather the things you may need when the time arises? Do you know when to work or study hard and when you need to rest? Have you planned for the future? Have you done your best in whatever you are doing at the moment? Are you studying hard to get a job in the future, to work hard for your savings, to serve God wholeheartedly for your 'heavenly investment'?

Do you know that effective planning saves hours of headache and worries? Planning ahead enables you to overcome hours of confusion and gives you enough energy to tackle tasks helping you to maximize your full potential to step into your desired future. Anybody who is addicted to planning is able to maintain focus on specific objectives and direct resources to the most important things in creating their sure future.

Know that whatever you do now will not be in vain, no matter how silly or unrelated it may be to you. Maybe you are working part time in a restaurant or maybe you are studying something that you think is unrelated to your course. Whatever it may be, God can always make something good out of it. You'll learn something that you would never have thought before without realizing it! Whatever it is, plan ahead.

BE DECISIVE

Every great leap forward in your life comes after you have made a clear decision of some kind. Decisiveness is about making a choice. A person who is decisive is able to make a clear distinction between options. In Deuteronomy 30:19, we read that God spoke through Moses to the children of Israel regarding their choice of decision. *'I call heaven and earth to record this day against you, that I have set before you life and death, blessing and cursing: therefore choose life, that both thou and thy seed may live:'*

Again in Joshua 1:8, we saw that Joshua was instructed to make the choice to meditate on the word of God for his success. '***This book of the law shall not depart out of thy mouth; but thou shalt meditate therein day and night, that thou mayest observe to do according to all that is written therein: for then thou shalt make thy way prosperous, and then thou shalt have good success.***'

Joshua 24:15, 'And if it seem evil unto you to serve the LORD, choose you this day whom ye will serve; whether the gods which your fathers served that were on the other side of the flood, or the gods of the Amorites, in whose land ye dwell: but as for me and my house, we will serve the LORD.'

The ants made a decision to prepare and gather food at the right time. They looked for and discovered the right moment for them to get out of their nests and hiding places to search for what was needful and important to their destiny. They were not too lazy to get out from their so-called 'comfort zone'. I am very sure that they were faced with fire and dangerous events which could have limited them from chasing their sure future. They were not hindered by the rocks, blocks, lizards, snakes and other things that could have posed a threat to them. The ants were fully determined to attain their destiny.

No power in the sky above or in the earth
below - indeed, nothing in all creation - will
ever be able to separate us from the love of God
that is revealed in Christ Jesus our Lord.

Romans 8:39

Are you always in your comfort zone, too lazy or scared to go out because your mind tells you that there is a lion in the street or snow on the road?

In Proverbs 22:13 the sluggard says, *'There is a lion outside! I shall be killed in the streets!'* My brothers and sisters in the Lord; do not be scared to try something that you have not done before. You can start to take on jobs that you have not done before. Take the step of faith and get into that field and take initiative like the ants. Each and every creature created by God is likely to face challenges, but we are urged by the word of God not to be dismay or discouraged. Ants are the most delicate because of their size, and are prone to being crushed as they are too small to notice. Therefore they can be trampled upon, but they were not scared to take chances to come out of their nests to achieve their goals and purpose.

**And there were four leprous men at the
entrance of the gate: and they said one to another,
why sit we here until we die?**

2 Kings 7:3

These were individuals who made a firm decision to get
up to pursue their destiny and not allow their leprosy to
hinder or limit them. They were determined that
whatever the case might be they were prepared to go and
get something. In those days, any person with such an
infectious disease must wear torn clothes, let his hair be
unkempt, cover the lower part of his face and cry out,
'Unclean! Unclean!' They did not allow public ridicule to

**The choice you make on a daily basis
affect what you will have, be or do in the
tomorrows of your life.**

It is very important that you do not postpone decisions
you must make today for your family, children, job,
marriage, relationship or future, because it could have
dire consequences on your future. Be decisive!

FOCUS ON YOUR ASSIGNMENT

Life is a journey which must be travelled with focus at all cost. You cannot get to your destination safely without focusing on the road to success. You cannot get to the mountain top without focus. The higher you climb the mountain of success the more you need to train your mind to focus. A pilot or a driver cannot get to where they are driving the people on board safely without deciding to remain focused.

From my field of work, you cannot be a surgeon or a nurse undertaking the responsibility of caring for patients without focusing on the particular patient allocated to you in the intensive care unit. This makes it clear that we all need the spirit of focus to enable us to overcome any limitations that may face us.

On the road to your destiny, you need to understand that there may be some obstacles and challenges. Jesus Christ and His disciples were faced with severe storms (Mark 6:45-56). This means that with the power of focus, you can achieve your dream. You only get to your destination or your future when you are willing to remain steadfast and focus.

Fight Obstacles Continuously Until you Succeed (FOCUS)

- Ferdinard S Lawson

You need to fight continuously until you succeed in life when you want to be a high achiever. When we examine the movement of an ant, we see that they all move in one direction irrespective of distraction.

Focusing on an assignment is very important in overcoming the habit of procrastination. We can observe that all ants focus on one thing, such as preparing and gathering food for the winter season. Are you equally focused on your God-given assignment? Remain focused and do not look at what is happening around you. It is necessary to search through yourself to see what actually takes your focus away from your assignment.

Be like the ants and do not give up easily. Successful people are never satisfied with their current level of achievement, neither are they limited by any form of disability. No matter what terrain they are going through, the ants keep on carrying the food without ever giving up. The Lord is on your side.

Success is a result of good decision making and failure is as a result of bad decision making-

Bishop Michael Hutton-Wood

DEVELOP SELF-DISCIPLINE

I head Bishop Michael Hutton-Wood once say 'self discipline is the ability to make yourself do what you should do, when you should do it, whether you feel like it or not'. Developing a spirit of self-discipline is actually mastering your self-confidence, self-esteem and inner strength, to produce self satisfaction. It is sometimes said that people with lack of self-discipline often becomes a failure. In view of this, it is possible to say that self-discipline is one of the ladders that will enable you to remain focused on your destiny.

When you look at the way an automobile works, many different parts are needed to make it sound and reliable. For example you need the gearbox, clutch, brakes, wheels, tyres, headlights, steering wheel and many other important parts, just to mention a few, to enable the car to function. So it is also vital that you have self-discipline as a vital part in your life to be able to overcome any limitation set before you.

**Self-discipline should be the fuel in your life
to get you to your destiny.**

This life is full of challenges, and sometimes this challenge tends to distract your focus and purpose for a particular day. However, when you are disciplined enough to remain on track you will surely get to that place of fulfillment. Imagine travelling on a highway (motorway) for a journey and you come across a number of lights indicating that you reduce your speed. You do not change your mind about the journey but will surely discipline yourself to continue it. The journey into your destiny will be obstructed by many roadworks, traffic lights and sometimes other drivers pulling in across you. It will take self-discipline to remain the driver you were when you first began the journey without getting upset and angry.

In my field of working, I have seen this demonstrated when an individual decide to quit smoking or other health-related habits like drinking and drug addiction; it takes self-discipline to overcome them. Do not allow the flood of procrastination to creep into your life or take you by surprise. Use these ladders to overcome the tsunami of procrastination. You are well able.

Discipline is the power that fuels the systems that LEAD you to larger goals. UNKNOWN

DEFICIENCY THREE:

TOXIC ASSOCIATIONS OR RELATIONSHIPS

Building great relationship takes time and energy. Many only discover how valuable such relationships are when they are tested. One author writes: 'Contouring your heart to beat with another requires extensive whittling to trim away self-centredness'. Some say that it's like riding the bus; if you are going to have company you must be willing to stop over to accommodate other people and the baggage they bring.

Any individual in your life influencing you negatively (ungodly counsels) should never be allowed to remain as a friend. In 2 Samuel 13:1-29, we were told how an individual person's kingship was destroyed just because of toxic friendship. Jonadab was Amnon's best friend and they had lived together for years, possibly sharing ideas, dreams, vision and goals. A time came when Jonadab needed advice from his so-called friend Amnon regarding his future. That one advice actually cost him his future as a king.

And it came to pass after this, that Absalom the son of David had a fair sister, whose name was Tamar; and Amnon the son of David loved her. And Amnon was so vexed, that he fell sick for his sister Tamar; for she was a virgin; and Amnon thought it hard for him to do anything to her. But Amnon had a friend, whose name was Jonadab, the son of Shimeah David's brother: and Jonadab was a very subtil man. And he said unto him, Why art thou, being the king's son, lean from day to day? wilt thou not tell me? And Amnon said unto him, I love Tamar, my brother Absalom's sister. And Jonadab said unto him, Lay thee down on thy bed, and make thyself sick: and when thy father cometh to see thee, say unto him, I pray thee, let my sister Tamar come, and give me meat, and dress the meat in my sight, that I may see it, and eat it at her hand.

So Amnon lay down, and made himself sick: and when the king was come to see him, Amnon said unto the king, I pray thee, let Tamar my sister come, and make me a couple of cakes in my sight, that I may eat at her hand. Then David sent home to Tamar, saying, Go now to thy brother Amnon's house, and dress him meat. So Tamar went to her brother Amnon's house; and he was laid down. And she took flour, and kneaded it, and made cakes in his sight, and did bake the cakes. And she took a pan, and poured them out before him; but he refused to eat. And Amnon said, Have out all men from me. And they went out every man from him. And Amnon said unto Tamar, Bring the meat into the chamber that I may eat of thine hand. And Tamar took the cakes which she had made, and brought them into the chamber to Amnon her brother. And when she had brought them unto him to eat, he took hold of her, and said unto her, come lie with me, my sister..'. The story continued.

This is the main reason why you need to be careful about those you allow into your life as friends. Any friendship that does not add to you, increase, appreciate, establish or multiply you but subtracts, makes life worse for you or brings failure should be cut off. It does not matter how long the friendship has been. You are safer breaking that friendship before your life is broken down alongside your health. Be open and frank with such 'toxic friends' and let them know that you cannot get anywhere with their negative influences in your life. Remember that such toxic friendships are like a car with punctured tyres. You cannot go anywhere until you change those tyres.

**Friendship is a choice you make which is
not legally demanded.**

Ferdinard S Lawson.

Who is the friend in your life that you share your dreams and ideas with? Whatever the case may be, you need to be very careful, because it could cost your destiny. In proverbs 18:24, Solomon said, 'there is a friend who sticks closer than a brother'. Relationship is about quality, not quantity. That is why heart connections can be so much stronger than blood connections when it comes to relationships. *'Can two walk together, except they be agreed? Amos 3:3 KJV.*

Any friendship void of agreement is 100% subject to lack of achievement in life.

Ferdinard S Lawson

Staying away from toxic relationships or friendships means that you have the responsibility to avoid relationships that may have a negative influence on your life and hinder you from getting to your destiny. You need to identify those people who may discourage you from your assignment in life, and avoid them completely.

It is very important to know that people you call friends are very necessary in achieving your purpose in life or destiny. They are either adding to you or subtracting from you. They are either making your life better or making it worse. You decide the types of friendship you want to keep or to avoid in order to get to your sure destiny.

'A righteous person is cautious with friendship,
but the way of the wicked leads them astray'

Proverbs 12: 26

To be able to overcome the limitations to destiny, it is crucial to take your time and assess the types of friendship you have in your life. If there are friends or relationship that regularly affect your productivities emotionally and sometimes affect your health, it is about time you decide to keep them or get rid of them completely to get to your sure future.

'People in our lives are like buttons in an elevator which takes us up to the top floor, keep us on the ground or in the basement.'

Bishop Michael Hutton-Wood

In Psalm 1:1, we are admonished not to even walk with them. 'Blessed is the man that walketh not in the counsel of the ungodly, nor standeth in the way of sinners, nor sitteth in the seat of the scornful'.

You must avoid the company of those people who do not in any way share your vision or have your interests at heart. You must do everything to protect and preserve your destiny. God has a purpose, a plan for you, and a brighter and greater future. This is why you must not allow negative people to sow seeds of discouragement in your life and distract you from God's divine purpose for you.

It is not easy to stay away from so-called friends, but my fellow believers, it will be in your best interests to do whatever you can to stay away from them. A negative individual or friend has the tendency to influence your character and behaviours - *'Birds of a feather flock together'*

Interestingly, you cannot actually determine the outcome of a relationship in terms of whether a friend will continue to remain the dependable and reliable individual he was when you first met. More often than not, it is not easy to identify any destructive friendship, but it is good to be aware of this possibility.

As you decide to overcome the things that hinder you from reaching your goals in life, it also vital to be aware of those friends who set themselves as negative critics in your life. These individuals could be limiting you by reminding you of your past mistakes and shortfalls.

'Now I beseech you, brethren, mark them which cause divisions and offences contrary to the doctrine which ye have learned; and avoid them. For they that are such serve not our Lord Jesus Christ, but their own belly; and by good words and fair speeches deceive the hearts of the simple.'

(Romans 16:17-18)

It is important that you treat people the same way you would like them to treat you. You need to see and assess the benefits of your friends in your life. Whatever the case each and every one of us needs friends in our lives. No one is an island, and never will be. We need friends who will help us get to our destiny and be willing to accommodate us during the good and the bad times.

Therefore these are the types of relationship or friendship you need in your life. You actually need a friend who will enable you and empower you to make good decisions regarding crucial moments in your life. Wouldn't you want a good friend to lift you up when you have fallen into the gutter?

Iron sharpeneth iron; so a man sharpeneth the countenance of his friend.

Proverbs 27:17 King James Bible (Cambridge Ed.)

When it comes to your achievement in life, there will also be different kinds of individual who will be attracted to you. These people can be classified as pilot friends, first-class friends and economy friends, determining your flight in life.

The Pilot friendships

These kinds of individuals are friends in your life serving as mentors and giving you speed in whatever you do. They board your friendship flight to motivate you, encourage you and sometimes take the ultimate responsibility to ensure that you achieve your dream. A pilot friend adds value to you and propels you to get to that sure goal that you have set for yourself. They share your vision and sometimes will go all the way to stay with you until you become all that God has made you to be. They never leave you along the way, regardless of your mistakes. They actually see great treasure in you and bring the gold out of you.

Remember that this kind of individual does not spy on you but is always there to celebrate your success. They are very concerned about your failures because they can see the greatness in your life and will go all the way to encourage you to get to the top. Pilot friends know your weaknesses. They will not remind you or dwell on the negative past or limit your progress in the pursuit of your dreams, but rather show your strengths, even in the midst of fearful events, to fortify your faith and free your spirit whenever there is anxiety. They do not leave you in mid air. They become your pillar in life.

First class friendships

These types of friends also gravitate toward you, simply because you share a vision with them. They only stay with you as long as they can get something from you. However, sometimes when situations get worse and things are not going the way they think they should, they get offended and give all kinds of excuses to stay away from you, even though they share the same vision with you. They have different agendas regarding the fulfillment of dreams and will only give you limited information as to what to do to achieve God's purpose for your life.

Economy friendships

Economy friendships are those which come into your life because of what you can give them to manage their lives. They do not add value to you but are always there to collect and receive from you. Although they also share your vision, they will not be happy if you are doing better than them. They will do everything possible to keep you in the same economy class. They are only happy for you as long as you remain at the economy level. When you decide to do something productive with your life, they will say things like 'We are all managing life here and now you are saying that you have to move on in life'. They will frustrate you from moving higher in life.

Even though you are thinking positive to remain focused on your assignment in life, these individuals will have negative ideas about you. You need to keep a positive attitude even when you are in the midst of these friends. Develop and establish defence mechanisms or boundaries to create your own happiness when you are around these toxic friends.

Toxic friends do not only limit themselves but the progress of people around them. They also cease to add value or contributions to the friendship you have with them and cause divisions between you and other productive friends who are willing to come into your life. Stay away from them.

Life is not built on selfishness and self-centredness; it's built on productive and relevant relationship.

DEFICIENCY FOUR: NEGATIVE THOUGHTS

'For from within, out of the heart of men, proceed evil thoughts, adulteries, fornications, murders, thefts, covetousness, wickedness, deceit, lasciviousness, an evil eye, blasphemy, pride, foolishness: All these evil things come from within, and defile the man.

Mark 7:21-23 King James Version (KJV)

Do you want to overcome the limitations to your destiny? Are your prepared to say boldly that there are no more limits to your destiny? Then you need to examine yourself and the thoughts that come to your mind daily. We all know that the devil plays a role in limiting us from getting to our sure destiny but it is also necessary that we check the very thoughts that flow in our mind.

You cannot conquer the devil until you conquer your thoughts

Ferdinard S Lawson.

Success life is about what you do with your life, because what you think determine your doings. You cannot be a successful person, overcoming the limitations of life, without thinking positively on what you do. The word of God says *'the way a man thinketh so shall he become'*. This is to say that you become what you think in life. Your thinking shapes your habits and behaviour.

Anyone who has the habit of procrastinating all the time will never live a life of fulfillment and cannot overcome the limitations of life. This is the main reason why you need to start adapting positive thinking.

From my book 'Igniting the power of your creative mind' you will discover that each and every one of us born into this world is influenced by the things we see, experiences which then determine the way we react to things around us. I have come to appreciate that our parents, our friends, our teachers, our bosses or marriage partners influence our thoughts ,knowingly or unknowingly.

According to T.D Jakes, once an individual has or develops certain thoughts in their mind, their mind start to send signals to their emotion which makes them take or make certain decisions or actions to produce the outcomes they see.

Brethren, I count not myself to have apprehended: but *this* one thing *I do*, forgetting those things which are behind, and reaching forth unto those things which are before, *Philippians 3:13*

It is very necessary to note that until an individual renews and changes his or her mind to remove negative backgrounds or experiences that affected them, their future and dreams are still going to control them, because our mind is influenced by negative thoughts from our background.

Everything we do is by choice and if you want to see a change in your personal life, then it is necessary that you change the way you view things until you are willing to renew your mind daily, minute by minute. Practise by changing the way your mind looks at everything with the word of God concerning your destiny. You will see little and your future will be controlled by those negative backgrounds.

'And do not be conformed to this world, but be transformed by the renewing of your mind, that you may prove what is that good and acceptable and perfect will of God.' *(Romans 12:2)*.

The secret of your future is hidden in your daily routine therefore be careful about what occupies your mind because it will greatly determine what you will become tomorrow:

Bishop Michael Hutton-Wood.

The terrible truth is that many of us, even though we are born again, spirit filled and Holy Ghost talking, still live in misery as a result of a negative background remaining in our minds, which pull us backwards.

Lack of renewing of mindset about negative experiences makes you depressed and can sometimes lead to suicidal thoughts. This is to say that being born again does not mean that you are going to prevent negative memories coming into your mind nor from having all those bad and depressing feelings. They are all still going to be there. That is why you need to renew your mind daily with the sure word of God.

Romans 12:1-2 teaches us what we must do: 'I beseech you therefore, brethren, by the mercies of God, that you present your bodies a living sacrifice, holy and acceptable to God. And do not be conformed to this world, but be transformed by the renewing of your mind, that you may prove to be what is good and acceptable and perfect in the will of God.'

When you were born again God gave you a brand new Godly heart, as it tells us in Ezekiel 36:26-27: 'Moreover, I will give you a new heart and put a new Spirit within you; and I will remove the heart of stone from your flesh and give you a heart of flesh. And I will put My Spirit within you'.

However, it is only when you combine that new heart with a brand new mindset that you will have awesome and incredible Godly changes taking place in your life and be on your way to success.

Remember that your mind is the thing that has control over every single action you take. Your mind controls your thoughts. Your mind tells your body exactly what to do. It tells your mouth what words to speak. It tells your eyes what to look at. It tells your ears what things to pay attention to and what things to tune out. It tells your brain what to think about. It tells your entire being how to respond in every single situation.

It is also vital that you renew your mindset each day with God's word against bad memory, depressing feelings and everything that takes your focus off God and places it on you and your problems.

Furthermore your mind is the foundation of your intellect, which really controls your personal self-esteem and drives you into success.

The way we use our minds is thinking. Therefore your life today is a result of what you thought of yesterday. It is very important that we really watch what goes through our minds especially the negative experiences that keep coming into your mind, and take control over it by renewing it daily.

It is true that sometimes we are all faced with some thoughts that we have no control over, but you can actually determine which ones dwell in your and control your lifestyle.

From the book 'How to negotiate your desired future with today's currency', by Bishop Michael Hutton-Wood, we discovered that the best way to deal with and forget about negative experiences is to become fruitful and occupy yourself with productive thinking to produce something positive.

Renewing your mind with the word of God concerning your destiny gives you assurance, which then promotes your confidence in your ability to pursue great things in life.

Your background of failures and shortcomings does not matter; when you begin to renew your mindset by changing the way you see yourself then you can embark on the road to achievement.

> **'Everyone has a past; but never allow your negative past to get in the way of your future.'**
>
> *Bishop Michael Hutton-Wood.*

God's promises are always assuring. He promised to be with us and never to forsake us, to gives us victory and rest (Exodus 33:14). Therefore there is no reason why you should feel intimidated by your negative conditions and not be bold enough to face life like Peter, who dared to walk on the waters.

A wise man once said 'when we sow in our weakness on our knees, we reap in strength on our feet'.

'Rejoice not against me, my enemies: when I fall, I shall arise; when I sit in darkness, the LORD shall be a light unto me.' Micah 7:8

> **'He who controls the past controls the future.'**
>
> *George Orwell, 1984.*

In other words, he who ignores the past is condemned to repeat it. So it is necessary that you discipline what goes through your mind (past) so as to move on.

Psalm 139 says 'I will praise the Lord, for I am fearfully and wonderfully made'. Encourage yourself by remembering that your birth was not an accident - you were not just born to add to the number of earth's population. The word of God says that you are a royal priesthood and a peculiar person. You are born to fill a gap and therefore you are unique. You have the mind of Christ and all it takes to be great. Just discover who you are in Christ and then you can recover your true self to accomplish greater things.

'For as a man thinketh in his heart, so is he'
Proverbs 23:7.

From the book 'Think like a Winner!' Dr Walter Staples writes: 'The key to success lies in your particular manner of thinking. When you change how you think about yourself, your relationships, your goals and your world, your life changes. If you change the quality of your thinking, you necessarily will change the quality of your life.'

Be very careful about what you allow to control your

mind. What you think about surely becomes your character and identity.

You will not struggle to excel in life and fulfill your purpose on earth in Jesus' name. Learn from the past by all means, but be like Apostle Paul: 'One thing I do, forgetting those things which are behind, and reaching forth unto those things which are before' - Philippians 3:13.

Remember also that no matter how hard you try, you cannot change the past, but definitely you can make a better future for yourself. Renewal of mind is a non-stop, continuous process. Paul says in Ephesians 4:23: 'Be renewed in the spirit of your mind'. We need to work our way through with our minds. The new man always contrasts the old lifestyle, therefore we must make every effort to renew our minds. We should make sure our minds think the way it is written in the Word of God. Or else, we need to work on it.

Romans 12:2 says, *'Be not conformed to this world but be transformed by the renewing of your mind'*. It is a commandment. Whenever the Bible says 'be', it is a commandment rather than a suggestion. We do not have a choice. The word 'conform' means to assume an outward expression that does not comes from an inward being. In other words, when you conform to something you feel so much influencing that you begin to change the way you act. When you begin to conform to this world system, you are not being faithful to who you really are on the inside. Behind the world system, there is the evil one.

'Transform' means to assume an outward expression that comes from the inward being. This transformation needs to take place in our minds. The Bible cautions us that the carnal mind in itself is enmity against God. The transformation comes from the word of God. When you get the word of God out of the pages of your Bible, read it and ponder over it, let it get into your mind and go down into your spirit. When we keep doing this, you can see your mind lining up to your spirit. This is the key. Otherwise, there is this constant battle that goes on between your mind and your spirit.

We are all eternal beings. We have an eternal spirit, we live in a mortal body and we have a soul that is made up of mind, will and emotions. The only doorway for the enemy into your soul is through your mind. Everything starts with a thought. Before you attempt to do anything, you think about it first. Your mind is the doorway to your deeds.

Proverbs 23:7 says: 'As a man thinks in his heart, so is he'. You cannot have a happy life if you have a sad mind. You need a healthy mind to start with. Our mind is the one that makes us the person God made us to be. Ephesians 6:12 says: 'We do not wrestle against flesh and blood, but against principalities, against powers, against the evil rulers of this dark world'.

It is so important to guard our mental lives. Isaiah 26:3 says: 'If you will keep your mind stayed on Me, I will hold you in perfect peace'. The situations and the circumstances change all the time. If our minds stay on the things that are changing day to day, our life will be like a boat in a storm. That is why it is so important we have an anchor. You will never wage a successful battle unless you have a personal relationship with the Lord Jesus Christ.

If you desire a meaningful and a successful life, then you must begin to renew your mind of the negative and embrace your future. These negatives or little foxes could be what are limiting you from getting to your destiny. *Take us the foxes, the little foxes that spoil the vines: for our vines have tender grapes.' Song of Solomon 2:15*

Life is never made unbearable by circumstances, only by lack of meaning and purpose.

Viktor Frankl

No matter what limited you in the past, or how poor, neglected or downtrodden your backgrounds were, you have what it takes to be at the top. It is my fervent prayer that as you begin to renew your mindset about your life you will be like the stars which do not struggle to shine and as a river which does not struggle to flow. You will get to your destiny.

Amen.

References

David B. Bohl
20 Qualities for a Successful Life

Bishop Prince Hampel
Dreams Direction Destiny, crossing the Rubicon of life.

John Maxwell
Developing the leadership within you

Bill Newman
The Power of Successful Life

Dr. Walter Staples

How to Think like a Winner

Bishop/Dr Michael Hutton-Wood)
Leadership Capsules
I Shall Rise Again
How to negotiate your desired future with today's currency
You need to do the ridiculous to experience the miraculous
175 Reasons why you cannot fail

David O Abioye books
Productive Thinking
Overcoming Stagnation

Dr David Oyedepo books
Understanding Vision
In pursuit of vision

Rhonda Jones
You Must Change Your Mind to Change Your Life

Mary Whelchel
Defeating Discouragement

Dragos Roua
100 ways to improve your life

Jemima Rayan
Become a winner

Steven Aitchison
100 ways To Develop your mind:
http://wealthmeaningoflife.blogspot.co.uk

www.ingramcontent.com/pod-product-compliance
Lightning Source LLC
Chambersburg PA
CBHW060137050426
42448CB00010B/2178